About the Author

Meet

Eve Bunting

Alice B. McGinty

The Rosen Publishing Group's
PowerKids Press™
New York

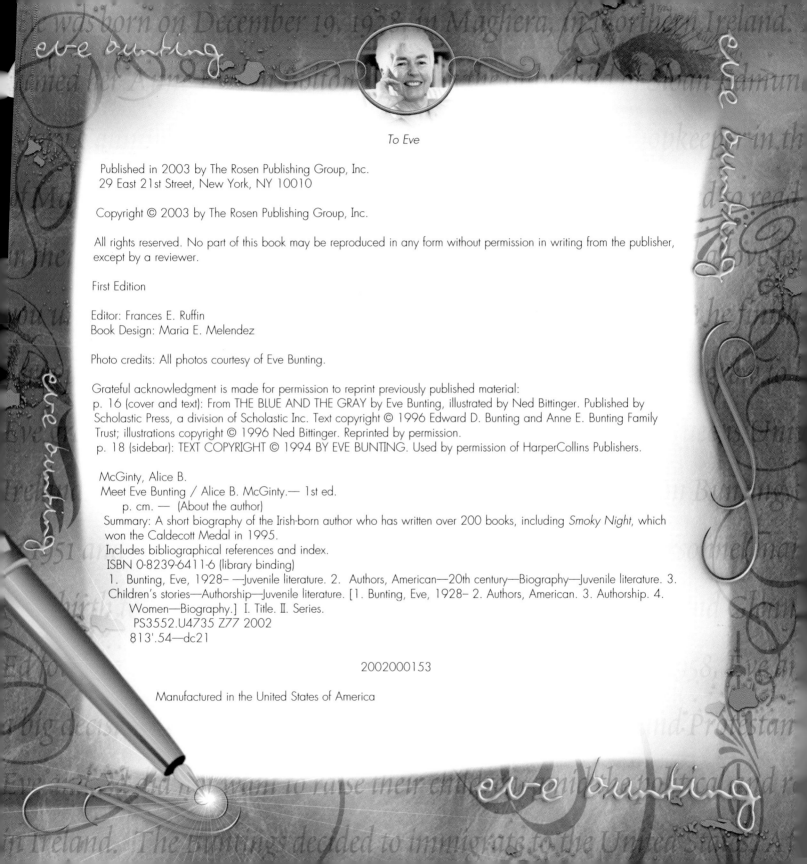

To Eve

Published in 2003 by The Rosen Publishing Group, Inc.
29 East 21st Street, New York, NY 10010

First Edition

Editor: Frances E. Ruffin
Book Design: Maria E. Melendez

Photo credits: All photos courtesy of Eve Bunting.

Grateful acknowledgment is made for permission to reprint previously published material:
p. 16 (cover and text): From THE BLUE AND THE GRAY by Eve Bunting, illustrated by Ned Bittinger. Published by Scholastic Press, a division of Scholastic Inc. Text copyright © 1996 Edward D. Bunting and Anne E. Bunting Family Trust; illustrations copyright © 1996 Ned Bittinger. Reprinted by permission.
p. 18 (sidebar): TEXT COPYRIGHT © 1994 BY EVE BUNTING. Used by permission of HarperCollins Publishers.

McGinty, Alice B.
  Meet Eve Bunting / Alice B. McGinty.— 1st ed.
      p. cm. — (About the author)
  Summary: A short biography of the Irish-born author who has written over 200 books, including *Smoky Night*, which won the Caldecott Medal in 1995.
  Includes bibliographical references and index.
  ISBN 0-8239-6411-6 (library binding)
  1. Bunting, Eve, 1928– —Juvenile literature. 2. Authors, American—20th century—Biography—Juvenile literature. 3. Children's stories—Authorship—Juvenile literature. [1. Bunting, Eve, 1928– 2. Authors, American. 3. Authorship. 4. Women—Biography.] I. Title. II. Series.
  PS3552.U4735 Z77 2002
  813'.54—dc21

                                  2002000153

    Manufactured in the United States of America

Contents

FZ 4230

Eve was born on December 19, 1928, in Maghera, in northern Ireland.

Between You and the Wind

When Eve Bunting was young, her father knew he couldn't always protect her from the real world, as much as he cared for her. He said, "Life is hard. I can't stand between you and the wind." Now Eve Bunting writes about real-life situations. Her books show children that life can be hard. In *Fly Away Home*, a homeless father and son live in an airport. *Smoky Night* tells of **riots** in the streets of Los Angeles in 1992. As did her father, Eve believes that adults can't always protect children from the real world. However, through her books, Eve offers children understanding and hope for the future.

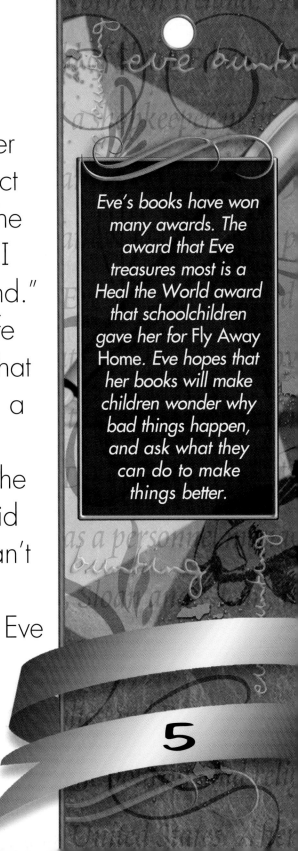

Eve's books have won many awards. The award that Eve treasures most is a Heal the World award that schoolchildren gave her for Fly Away Home. Eve hopes that her books will make children wonder why bad things happen, and ask what they can do to make things better.

◁ Eve was born in Ireland. This photo shows Eve and her father, Sloan Edmund Bolton.

A Small Town in Northern Ireland

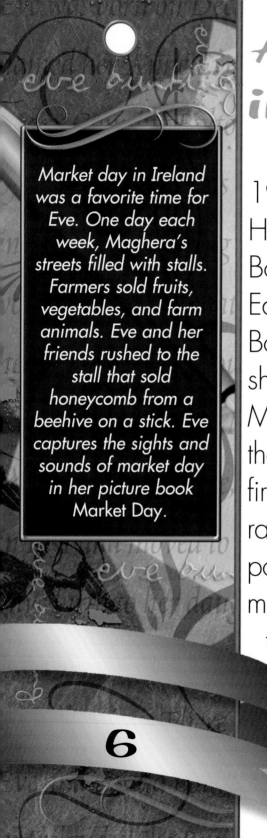

Market day in Ireland was a favorite time for Eve. One day each week, Maghera's streets filled with stalls. Farmers sold fruits, vegetables, and farm animals. Eve and her friends rushed to the stall that sold honeycomb from a beehive on a stick. Eve captures the sights and sounds of market day in her picture book Market Day.

Eve was born on December 19, 1928, in Maghera, Northern Ireland. Her parents named her Anne Evelyn Bolton. She was the only child of Sloan Edmund Bolton and Mary Canning Bolton. Sloan was the postmaster and a shopkeeper in the small town of Maghera. He was an important man there. Eve's family liked to read by the fireplace in their home during Ireland's rainy weather. Eve's father had a love for poetry. "Do you understand what that means, Darlin'?" he'd ask Eve when he finished reading her a poem. Eve thought the words he read were beautiful. She grew to love poetry.

This photo was taken of three-year-old Eve during a vacation in Portrush, Northern Ireland. ▷

eve bunting

Maghera★
Belfast
Northern Ireland

Great Britain

Sunderland

Dublin ●

Ireland

London ●

Cork ●

eve bunting

eve bunting

eve bunting

eve bunting

eve bunting

Off to School

When Eve was seven, she was sent to the Methodist College boarding school in Belfast, Northern Ireland. She lived in a **dormitory** with 12 other girls. The students attended classes, studied, and ate meals together. Eve often got homesick. **World War II** was being fought in Europe. Sometimes German planes bombed the city. The students hid in underground bomb shelters and carried gas masks. Eve made close friends, and they helped one another through these hard times. She later wrote the book *Spying on Miss Müller*, based on her years in boarding school. Eve enjoyed writing **essays**, poems, and stories.

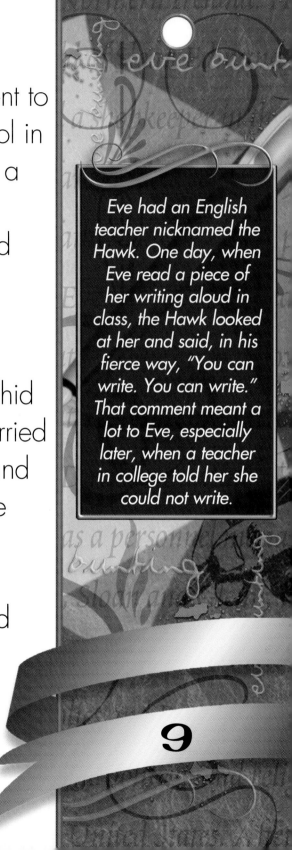

Eve had an English teacher nicknamed the Hawk. One day, when Eve read a piece of her writing aloud in class, the Hawk looked at her and said, in his fierce way, "You can write. You can write." That comment meant a lot to Eve, especially later, when a teacher in college told her she could not write.

◁ *Eve, during her boarding school days, is the girl on the far right in the first row.*

Moving On

Eve graduated from Methodist College in 1945 and entered Queens University in Belfast, Northern Ireland. While there, she met fellow student Edward Davison Bunting. They married in 1951. Eve gave birth to her daughter, Christine, then to her sons, Sloan and Glenn. For a while, they lived in Scotland where Ed worked as a **personnel manager**. The family moved back to Belfast when Ed found a job there. In 1958, Eve and Ed made a big decision. There was much hatred between **Catholics** and **Protestants** in Belfast. Eve and Ed did not want to raise their children amid the political and religious troubles in Northern Ireland. The Buntings decided to move to the United States.

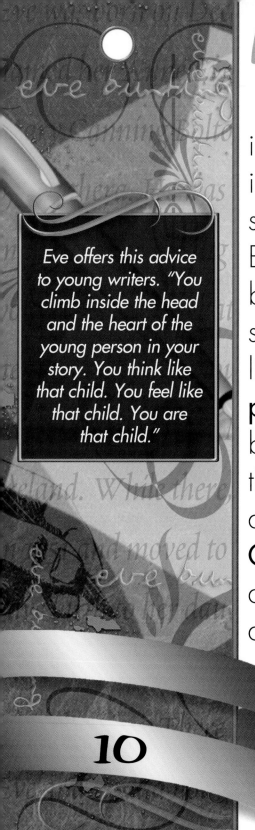

Eve offers this advice to young writers. "You climb inside the head and the heart of the young person in your story. You think like that child. You feel like that child. You are that child."

Eve and husband Ed are shown dancing at a party. Inset: *Eve's children, Sloan, Christine, and* ▷ *Glenn, at their home in Pasadena, California.*

The Land of Opportunity

Eve, Ed, and their three young children arrived in America with no money and no jobs. However, they saw America as the land of opportunity. They settled in California. Eve was lonely, though. She missed her mother and her friends in Ireland. It had been a hard decision to leave her country. After about a year, Ed found a job in Los Angeles as a hospital **administrator**. The family bought a home on a tree-lined street in Pasadena, California. Eve stayed busy raising her children. She also took classes to study U.S. history and the **Constitution**. Eve become a citizen in 1968.

Eve and her family moved into this home in Pasadena after they moved to America. She and Ed have lived there ever since.

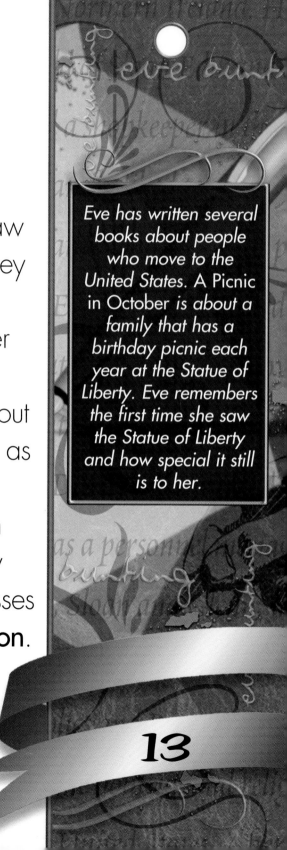

Eve has written several books about people who move to the United States. *A Picnic in October* is about a family that has a birthday picnic each year at the Statue of Liberty. Eve remembers the first time she saw the Statue of Liberty and how special it still is to her.

Writing for Publication

Eve is shown at her desk writing a new story. Her first book, The Two Giants, was published in 1972.

With Ed and her teenage children gone all day at work or at school, Eve faced long days in an empty house. She took a writing for publication course that was offered at Pasadena City College. "It was the best decision I ever made," she later said. Eve turned a small room in her attic into a writing room. She wrote poems and short stories and sold two to children's magazines. Then Eve remembered an Irish tale about two giants. "I thought everybody in the world knew that story," Eve says. Many people didn't know the story. She rewrote the tale and made it a book. She called her book *The Two Giants*.

Eve shows her book, So Far from the Sea, *and the dolls that resemble the people in the story.* ▷

ve was born on December 19, 1928, in Maghera, in Northern Ireland.

So far from the Sea

by Eve Bunting

Illustrated by Chris K. Soentpiet

The Buntings decided to immigrate to the United States.

The BLUE and the GRAY

BY Eve Bunting   ILLUSTRATED BY Ned Bittinger

■ SCHOLASTIC

In 1862 this was a battleground,
and here two armies fought
and soaked the grass with blood.
I guess the flowers were red instead
of white that night.
It was the Civil War,
The North against the South,
The blue against the gray.
White against black.
White against white.
Us against us,
To tell it right.
My dad says that's the saddest kind
of war there is,
though every war is sad
and most are bad.
—From The Blue and the Gray
(1996)

Following the Wind

After *The Two Giants* was **published** in 1972, Eve found ideas for her books everywhere. Most ideas come from the news. Eve reads several newspapers and magazines every day. She thinks about what is going on in the world and how it might affect children. Eve wrote *Someday a Tree* after reading an article about a tree that had been poisoned. When there were riots in Los Angeles in 1992, Eve wondered what it was like for the children who lived close by. This gave her the idea for *Smoky Night.* Hearing teachers talk about a class trip to the **Vietnam Memorial** gave Eve the idea for *The Wall.* Eve also has written many books about holidays. She and her children especially love Halloween.

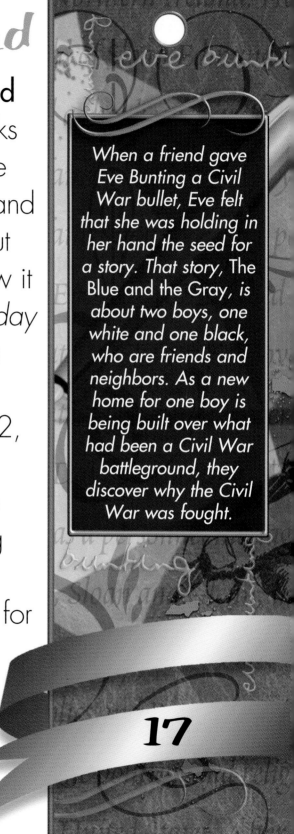

When a friend gave Eve Bunting a Civil War bullet, Eve felt that she was holding in her hand the seed for a story. That story, The Blue and the Gray, *is about two boys, one white and one black, who are friends and neighbors. As a new home for one boy is being built over what had been a Civil War battleground, they discover why the Civil War was fought.*

The Serious and the Silly

Some adults think that the subjects of Eve's books are too difficult or scary for children. However, Eve knows that many children will live through hard times, just as she did. Her books can help children to understand serious problems. Eve's **editors** support her. They have never turned down a book because adults might think the theme is too difficult. Eve also writes about silly, fun subjects. Eve's books, both serious and silly, have won many awards. She is proud of *Nasty, Stinky Sneakers* because it has won many awards voted on by children. *Smoky Night* won the 1995 Caldecott Medal, an award given to the best picture book for children.

> "Colin stared down at himself. His blue knit shirt with the alligator on the pocket that his aunt Noni had said made his eyes look bluer had turned a strange, blotchy purple. The warm air and the running had dried his jeans. Now they were coated with scum like the skin on a parched mud puddle. He bent his knee and the scum cracked, little pieces dropping off. 'Then Jack's sneakers accidentally got dumped in the garbage,'" Webster butted in.
> —from Nasty, Stinky Sneakers (1994)

18

Eve attends writers conferences. In these photos she's examining art from her book So Many Monsters, and receiving an award.

Eve was born on December 19, 1928, in Maghera, in Northern Ireland. ... named her Anne Evelyn Bolton. She was the only child of ...

eve bunting

... here was much hatred between Catholics and Protestants ... did not want to raise their children ... in Ireland. The Boltons decided to immigrate to the United States ...

A World Filled with Ideas

Eve and Ed still live in the same house in Pasadena, with a swimming pool and a flower garden in the backyard. When their children grew up and moved away, Eve moved her office to a room downstairs. Eve's world is still filled with ideas. As soon as she finishes one book, she begins the next. She writes using a pencil and notebook. When her story is done, she types it on her computer. Eve loves to create new stories. Eve has written and published more than 200 books. She is active in writers' groups, and she has taught a writing class at Pasadena City College.

◁ *Eve and Ed Bunting posed for this picture with their children and grandchildren. When she isn't working, Eve plays golf and visits her four granddaughters, all of whom live in California.*

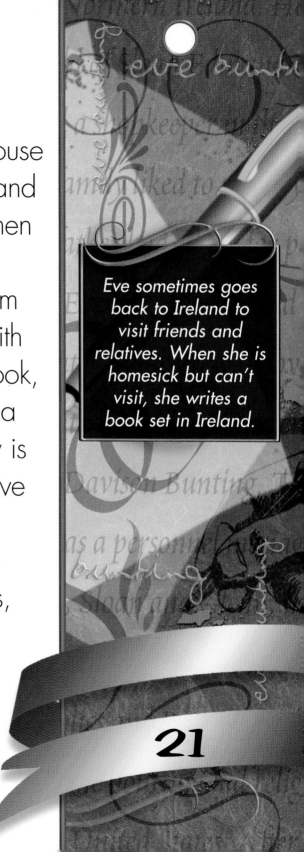

Eve sometimes goes back to Ireland to visit friends and relatives. When she is homesick but can't visit, she writes a book set in Ireland.

In Her Own Words

Eve Bunting at age four with a favorite doll.

When did you know that you wanted to be a writer?
I didn't know I wanted to be a writer until I was over 40 years old. My children were all teenagers.

Why did you decide to focus on writing for children?
I tried first some adult stories and realized I was more at ease with children's stories.

How is writing for children different from writing for adults?
Writing for children seems to me to be more honest and straightforward than writing for adults.

What life experiences do you draw on for your writing?
I like to listen to my children (grown now!) and grandchildren. I like to use other people's experiences that interest me that I read about or hear about.

Which books did you enjoy reading as a child?
My favorite books were the Anne of Green Gables series. I liked to pretend I was Anne! I also liked poetry a lot and adventure stories such as *The Swiss Family Robinson* and *Treasure Island*.

What do your young readers tell you that they like most about your books?
The children tell me they like funny books such as *Nasty, Stinky Sneakers* or *Wanna Buy an Alien?* They also like to have their hearts touched by some of the more emotional books I write such as *Fly Away Home* or *So Far from the Sea*, for example.

Glossary

administrator (ad-MIH-nih-stray-ter) One who directs or manages something.

Catholics (KATH-liks) People who belong to the Roman Catholic religion.

Constitution (kahn-stih-TOO-shun) The basic rules by which the United States is governed.

dormitory (DOR-mih-tor-ee) A large building where many people live together.

editors (EH-dih-terz) The people who correct errors, check facts, and decide what will be printed in a newspaper, book, or magazine.

essays (EH-sayz) Short pieces of writing that feature personal points of view.

personnel manager (per-sun-EL MA-nih-jer) Someone who manages the accounts of people who work for a company.

Protestants (PRAH-tihs-tunts) People who belong to a Christian-based religion, but are not Catholic.

published (PUH-blishd) When something such as a book, story, or poem has been printed so that people can read it.

riots (RY-uts) Disturbances caused by large groups of people.

Vietnam Memorial (vee-it-NAHM meh-MOR-ee-ul) A wall built to remember the American soldiers who died fighting in the Vietnam War (1954–1975).

World War II (WURLD WOR TOO) The war fought from 1939 to 1945. The United States, Great Britain, the Soviet Union, and their allies were on one side. Germany, Italy, Japan, and their allies were on the other side.

Index

B

Belfast, Northern Ireland, 9–10

C

Caldecott Medal, 18

F

Fly Away Home, 5, 22

M

Maghera, Northern Ireland, 6

N

Nasty, Stinky Sneakers, 18, 22

P

Pasadena, California, 13, 21

S

Scotland, 10
Smoky Night, 5, 17–18
So Far from the Sea, 22
Someday a Tree, 17

Spying on Miss Müller, 9

T

Two Giants, The, 14, 17

V

Vietnam Memorial, 5, 17

W

Wall, The, 5, 17
Wanna Buy an Alien?, 22
World War II, 9

Web Sites

Due to the changing nature of Internet links, PowerKids Press has developed an online list of Web sites related to the subject of this book. This site is updated regularly. Please use this link to access the list:

www.powerkidslinks.com/aa/evebun/

24